TIMELINE OF GEORGE HANDEL'S LIFE

1685 George Frideric Handel is born in Halle, Germany.

1689 George teaches himself to play music on a clavichord, a small keyboard instrument.

1692 George travels with his father to the court of the Duke of Saxe-Weissenfels. After hearing George play the organ, the duke tells Mr. Handel to get his son music lessons.

1694 George studies the organ with Friedrich Zachow, one of Halle's best music teachers.

1702 George enters the University of Halle. He is offered the position of organist in one of Halle's many churches.

1703 George travels to Hamburg. He meets Johann Matteson, a well-known musician, who Handel will one day challenge to a sword fight! George joins the Hamburg Theater orchestra, where he plays the violin and harpsichord.

1706 George visits Florence, Rome, Naples, and Venice.

THIS WAY

UP HERE

1710 Handel returns to Germany, where he is appointed choirmaster to the Elector of Hanover. George makes his first trip to London, England. He soon makes London his permanent home.

1714 When the Queen of England dies, Handel's old boss, the Elector of Hanover, travels to London to become the new King of England.

1717 George Handel performs his *Water Music* for the king during a boat parade celebration.

1718 -1736 Handel composes dozens of new pieces, including cantatas, organ concertos, operas, and oratorios.

1737 George starts having mysterious medical problems. He loses the use of his right hand for six weeks!

1742 Handel travels to Dublin to perform the *Messiah*.

1749 Handel composes *Music for the Royal Fireworks*.

1759 George Frideric Handel dies in London.

GETTING TO KNOW
THE WORLD'S
GREATEST COMPOSERS

GEORGE
HANDEL

WRITTEN AND ILLUSTRATED BY MIKE VENEZIA

CONSULTANT
DONALD FREUND, PROFESSOR OF COMPOSITION,
INDIANA UNIVERSITY SCHOOL OF MUSIC

CHILDREN'S PRESS®

An Imprint of Scholastic Inc.

Picture Acknowledgements
Photographs ©: cover and title page: Stock Montage; 3: Anonymous, Portrait of Friedrich
Handel, Accademia Rossini, Bologna, Italy, Giraudon/Art Resource, NY; 4 left: Rischgitz/
Getty Images; 4 right: Oliviero, Domenico, Interior of Teatro Regio. Museo Civico, Turin, Italy.
Scala/Art Resource, NY; 5: English School/Getty Images; 6: North Wind Picture Archives; 7:
INTERFOTO/Alamy Images; 12: North Wind Picture Archives; 15 left: Warburg/Wikimedia;
15 right: Bibliotheque Nationale de France; 18-19: Canaletto. Lo sposalizio del mare, Museo
Pushkin, Moscow. Scala/Art Resource, NY; 21: Universal Images Group/Getty Images; 24:
Hulton Archive/Getty Images; 25: North Wind Picture Archives; 26-27: Canaletto, View of
London from the Thames. National Gallery, Prague, Czech Republic. Giraudon/Art Resource,
NY; 32: Stock Montage.

Library of Congress Cataloging-in-Publication Data

Names: Venezia, Mike, author, illustrator.
Title: George Handel / written and illustrated by Mike Venezia ; consultant,
   Donald Freund.
Description: Revised edition. | New York, NY : Children's Press, 2018. |
   Series: Getting to know the world's greatest composers | Includes
   bibliographical references and index.
Identifiers: LCCN 2017048072| ISBN 9780531228708 (library binding) | ISBN
   9780531233733 (pbk.)
Subjects: LCSH: Handel, George Frideric, 1685-1759--Juvenile literature. |
   Composers--Biography--Juvenile literature.
Classification: LCC ML3930.H25 V46 2018 | DDC 780.92 [B] --dc23 LC record available at
https://lccn.loc.gov/2017048072

Scholastic Inc., 557 Broadway, New York, NY 10012.

1 2 3 4 5 6 7 8 9 10 R 27 26 25 24 23 22 21 20 19 18

A portrait of George Frideric Handel

George Frideric Handel was one of the most famous composers in Europe during the 1700s. He traveled all over Germany and Italy, learning as much as he could about the music of the day. In 1712, George Handel moved to London, England. There he spent the rest of his life composing some of the greatest music ever written.

A concert of sacred music in a German cathedral in the 1700s

An Italian opera theater in the 1700s

In Germany, George Handel learned about choir music and organ music, which were played in the many churches there. In Italy, where opera was invented, he learned how songs could be performed beautifully by a single great singing star. He also learned how orchestra music was composed.

VUE des FEUX d'ARTIFICE et des ILLUMINATIONS donnés par Monseigneur le Duc de RICHMOND de LENOX et d'AUBIGNY. sur la TAMISE, et vis a vis de son Hotel. Lundi le 15.me de Mai 1749. Sous la direction de Mons. Frederic.

In 1749, to celebrate the signing of an important English peace treaty, Handel composed music for a special fireworks display in Green Park, London.

In England, George learned about important-sounding royal music, which was used to celebrate an event or honor a king or queen. George Handel often combined the different musical styles he had studied, and included them in his most famous musical pieces.

George Frideric Handel was born in the
German town of Halle in 1685. Halle was a
lively town while George was growing up.
It had lots of places where he could hear
music. Organ recitals and choir music were
performed at the town's many churches.
Town musicians played brass instruments

German street
musicians of
the 1700s

for special occasions, and Halle had lots
of street musicians, too. George Frideric
Handel also got to meet many interesting
people when he was little. People from all
over the world came to see his father, who
was a well-known barber-surgeon.

s strange as it seems today, during the 1600s and 1700s, barbers not only cut hair, but also were trained as doctors and operated on people!

George loved music from the time when he was very young. Unfortunately, his father didn't care for it at all. Mr. Handel

thought music was a waste of time, and that
musicians could never make a good living.
He didn't want George to study music or
ever play an instrument. There is a story
that tells how George's mother and aunt
helped smuggle a harpsichord into the attic
so George could practice quietly at night.

Whether the harpsichord story is true or not, George somehow learned to play music all by himself. When he was ten years old, his father took him along on a trip to the palace of the Duke of Weissenfels. While Mr. Handel went about his business, George found an organ in the duke's chapel and began to play it. The duke happened to be passing by and could hardly believe his ears. He had never heard such beautiful music being played by such a young boy.

The duke tried to convince Mr. Handel that his talented son deserved a chance to study music. A soon as he got back home, George began taking music lessons.

An old engraving of the German city of Hamburg

George learned quickly from his teacher, Friedrich Zachow, who was one of the best organists in Germany. George became an expert organ and harpsichord player, and began composing music. He also learned to play the violin and oboe.

George loved music so much that he decided to make it his career. When he was seventeen years old, he began traveling to other German cities that were known as important music centers. His first stop was Hamburg, where he got a job as a violinist and harpsichord player with the city's opera orchestra.

Operas were the top entertainment in Europe during Handel's time. They were as popular as movies are today. People loved to spend evenings listening to the great singers and watching them act out a story with beautiful costumes and scenery.

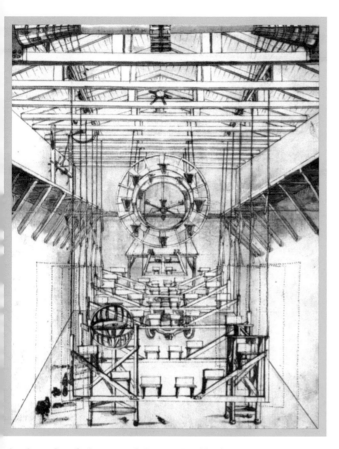

A sketch of the machinery built for an opera stage set of the 1700s

A sketch showing how the same stage set would look during the actual opera performance

They couldn't wait to find out what special effects the stage designers would come up with next. Sometimes the designers built machines that were able to show volcanos, or shipwrecks, or strange, supernatural scenes.

While he was in Hamburg, George met a talented singer and composer named Johann Matteson.

Johann and George became the best of friends, and helped each other with their music. Once, however, they had a serious argument and got into a duel with swords! The argument started when both of them wanted to play the harpsichord during an opera that Johann had written. George

Handel could be very stubborn, especially
when it came to music. Fortunately, no one
was seriously hurt during the fight, and
George and Johann soon became friends
again. In fact, Johann helped George write
his first opera. It was called *Almira*, and it
became a big hit right away.

Lo sposalizio del mare,
a view of Venice by 18th-century
Italian artist Canaletto

George was happy about his success, but decided to leave Germany and go to Italy to learn more about opera. Italian operas were the most popular type in Europe. Italy had more opera houses and great singers than anywhere else in the world. While living there, George met—and studied the music of—such famous composers as Alessandro Scarlatti and Arcangelo Corelli. In Venice, Italy, George composed his first Italian opera. It became a big hit, too.

George Frideric Handel started to become famous all over Europe. In 1710, the ruler of the German state of Hanover, Georg Ludwig, heard about Handel. He asked him to head up his royal music department. George accepted the job, but soon after asked to be excused so he

Southwark Fair, an engraving showing a London street scene, by 18th-century English artist William Hogarth

could travel to London, England, where he had been invited to write operas. During the 1700s, England was behind the rest of Europe when it came to opera. People there were anxious to see and hear Italian operas—like the ones George Frideric Handel was writing.

During his first few years in England, George Handel wrote many successful operas. He was even able to start his own opera company. But then, something happened. Slowly, people began losing interest in operas. The English people were becoming tired of listening to Italian songs they couldn't understand and stories that were usually

very complicated. Many of the opera stars had become spoiled, and demanded huge amounts of money to sing. Sometimes they even got into fights right on the stage. George Handel started losing money, and had to close his company. He became discouraged, but didn't give up. Handel started composing a different kind of music that he hoped his audience would enjoy more.

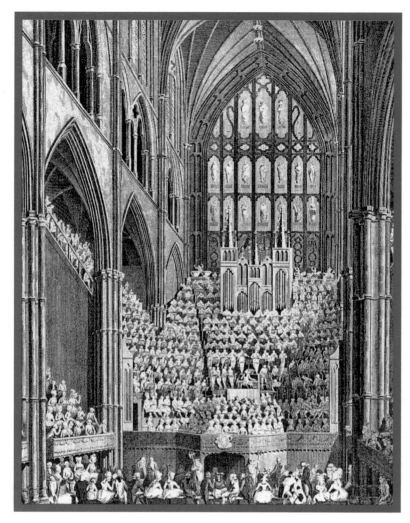

A performance of one of George Handel's oratorios at London's Westminster Abbey

George Handel began writing oratorios. An oratorio is similar to an opera, except that a chorus, instead of one or two great singing stars, sings most of the music. Also, oratorios don't have acting, costumes, or scenery.

Usually, George Handel wrote his oratorios about exciting stories from the Bible. The songs were sung in English, so that everyone in London could understand what was going on.

Singers in Handel's oratorios in London

People loved Handel's new music. One reason his oratorios became so popular was that Handel had a special talent for creating music that helps you picture a story in your mind. Part of a famous Handel oratorio called *Israel in Egypt* tells how Moses, with the help of God, sent millions of flies to irritate the Egyptian pharaoh. Moses did this to convince the pharaoh to stop using the people of Israel as slaves.

The high voices of the women chorus members and the quick rhythm of the violins used in the piece lets you almost see and feel pesty flies swarming all over the place!

Handel also composed music just for instruments. It's easy to picture the excitement and grandness of a royal boat party in his most famous orchestra work, *Water Music*. Handel wrote *Water Music* for his old boss, Georg Ludwig of Germany, who had become George I, King of England, in 1714.

Handel wrote *Water Music* for a grand royal concert on London's Thames River in 1717. While King George I floated along on his royal barge, Handel conducted 50 musicians on a nearby boat!

George Frideric Handel's most famous piece is an oratorio called *Messiah*. It is about the life of Jesus Christ. The words that are sung to it come right out of the Bible. *Messiah* was first performed in Dublin, Ireland. It was written to help raise money for poor people, the same way many charity concert performances do today.

Handel felt deeply inspired when he wrote his most famous work. He used everything he had learned in the past. When you listen to *Messiah*, you can hear a combination of Italian opera-style singing, English orchestral music, and German church music. The piece also includes many different moods, from very happy to very solemn.

So many people in Dublin were anxious to hear *Messiah* that newspapers there printed up ads asking women not to wear their usual hooped skirts and men not to wear swords. They wanted to make sure there was room for everyone in the music hall.

Even though *Messiah* was very successful
in Ireland, it didn't go over very well
back in London. Church leaders there
didn't like the idea of having any kind of
entertainment about the life of Jesus. They
tried to convince people that *Messiah* was
disrespectful, and that they shouldn't see it.
    George decided it might be better to

perform his oratorio just once a year, for charity. George Frideric Handel was a very generous person. He donated lots of his time to raise money for poor people. His favorite charity was the foundling hospital. The foundling hospital took care of babies who had no parents. For many years, Handel performed his *Messiah* right at the hospital.

A festival celebrating George Handel's music
was held at London's Crystal Palace in 1862.

In April of 1759, after giving a performance of *Messiah*, George Frideric Handel became ill. He died eight days later, at the age of seventy-four. Even though he composed many well-loved operas, oratorios, and orchestra pieces, *Messiah* was his favorite. Eventually, *Messiah* became appreciated in London. Today, it is considered one of the world's great music masterpieces.

It's pretty easy to find Handel's music on the radio or online for free. At holiday time, some cities put on special performances of *Messiah* in which the public is invited to join the chorus.

LEARN MORE BY TAKING THE HANDEL QUIZ!

(ANSWERS ON THE NEXT PAGE.)

1. In 1703, Dietrich Buxtehude, a famous musician in Lubeck, Germany, offered his position as town organist to George Handel. Why did Handel turn down this important job?
- **a** Buxtehude's deal didn't include a decent insurance or vacation plan.
- **b** Handel would have to marry Buxtehude's daughter if he accepted the job.
- **c** Handel would have to take over the monthly payments on Buxtehude's very expensive organ.

2. Handel was so busy writing music and conducting, he didn't have much time for hobbies. What was the one thing he did find time to enjoy?
- **a** Competing in bocce ball tournaments
- **b** Collecting art
- **c** Participating on the Thames River swim team

3. George Handel was known to be quick-tempered and easily annoyed. Aside from getting into a sword fight with his friend over a disagreement, what else would cause Handel to show his fierce temper?
- **a** When every instrument in his orchestra wasn't tuned properly
- **b** When opera singers would dare to disagree with him
- **c** When anyone was late to his concert
- **d** All of the above

4. TRUE OR FALSE: Handel was a perfectionist and worked very slowly. He would spend months, if not years, writing an opera or oratorio.

ANSWERS

1. **b** Dietrich Buxtehude's deal included the marrying of his daughter, Margreta. Handel didn't care that much for Margreta, plus he wasn't ready to get married, so he turned the job down.

2. **b** Handel loved art and collected paintings for his home. He owned a number of prints and at least 70 paintings, one of which may have been a Rembrandt landscape!

3. **d** Handel did have a short fuse and explosive temper. Most people forgave him, though, because he also had a fun sense of humor and was very generous. Most importantly, George Handel gave people what they loved most, which was beautiful music.

4. **FALSE** Handel was an incredibly speedy composer. He composed *Messiah* in about three weeks. This was pretty amazing, since he wrote 260 pages of music, creating parts for a chorus and orchestra in a piece that's over two hours long!